Reach for the Skies

Sarah Fleming

OXFORD

UNIVERSITY PRESS

OXFORD
UNIVERSITY PRESS

Great Clarendon Street, Oxford OX2 6DP

Oxford University Press is a department of the University of Oxford.
It furthers the University's objective of excellence in research, scholarship,
and education by publishing worldwide in

Oxford   New York

Auckland   Cape Town   Dar es Salaam   Hong Kong   Karachi
Kuala Lumpur   Madrid   Melbourne   Mexico City   Nairobi
New Delhi   Shanghai   Taipei   Toronto

With offices in

Argentina   Austria   Brazil   Chile   Czech Republic   France   Greece
Guatemala   Hungary   Italy   Japan   Poland   Portugal   Singapore
South Korea   Switzerland   Thailand   Turkey   Ukraine   Vietnam

Oxford is a registered trade mark of Oxford University Press
in the UK and in certain other countries

British Library Cataloguing in Publication Data

Data available

ISBN 978-0-19-917942-8

9   10   8

Printed in China by Imago

Paper used in the production of this book is a natural,
recyclable product made from wood grown in sustainable forests.
The manufacturing process conforms to the environmental
regulations of the country of origin.

Acknowledgements

The publisher would like to thank the following for permission to reproduce
photographs: **p4** Corbis/Manuel Blondeau/Photo & Co, **p5** Corbis/Mike Finn-Kelcey, **p7**b
Corbis/Bettmann, t Mary Evans Picture Library, **p8**t Corbis/Bettmann, cl & cr Corbis/Gianni Dagli
Orti, **p9**t Science & Society Picture Library/Science Museum, **p10** & **11** Empics, **p13**b Empics,
t Getty/Time & Life Pictures/Dana Frank, **p14** Getty/Hulton Archive, **p15**t Getty/Peter
Macdiarmid, b Fotopress/Ross Setford, **p16**t Corbis/Reuters, b Kobal, **p17**t Topfoto/Roger-Viollet,
b Corbis/Underwood & Underwood, **p18**b Getty/Brian Bahr, t Getty/AFP, **p19**t Getty/Phil Cole,
b Corbis/Yannis Behrakis/Reuters, **p20** Corbis/Reuters, **p22**t Corbis/Reuters, c Action Plus, b
Getty/Gary M Prior, **p22**t Bridgemand Art Library/Samuel Courthauld Trust, Courthauld Institute
of Art Gallery, b Bridgeman Art Library/Museum of Modern Art, New York, **p23**t Smithsonian
Institute, b Getty/AFP/John McHugh, **p24** & **25** Dr Temple Grandin, **p27** Corbis/Reuters

Cover photography by: Getty Images/Phil Cole & Corbis/Reuters

Illustrations by: **p26** Barking Dog Art, **p6/7**, **p12**, **p26** (inset) Greg Becker, **p4** Andy Hamilton

The publisher would like to thank Dr Temple Grandin for her generosity in providing material on her work

Design by Bigtop Design Ltd

Contents

Use the Glossary of conditions on pages 28–30 to find out about different illnesses and diseases. Throughout the book these conditions are written in **blue**.

Introduction

Deciding on a career is hard for almost everybody. We tend to choose something that we might not only enjoy, but that we also think we might be good at.

Even within a career like professional rugby, you need people with different skills and body shapes.

Front row: big, strong, muscular

Backs: small, wiry, fast

We are not all born the same.
We all have different abilities and skills.

Our bodies are different. High achievers recognise their abilities and work hard at them. Some people manage to do this *even if* their problems are harder than most people's.

Diseases, illnesses or **conditions** can restrict our choices. But if we play to our strengths, they don't have to.

Paula Radcliffe (UK 1973-)

Paula Radcliffe, the British **athlete**, has held 11 world records during her running career.

> "I don't really think **asthma** has affected my career – if anything it's made me more determined to be successful and reach my maximum potential."

Conditions, illnesses and diseases can stop people from daring to set themselves ambitious goals. But some people manage to concentrate on their strengths, and some don't see their weaknesses as problems at all.

This book looks at some of these people and the careers they have chosen.

Paula Radcliffe

Born: Northwich, UK, 17 December 1973

1986: In her first national race, an under-12 cross country, Radcliffe finished 299th. She is now arguably the best ever long-distance runner in the world

1992: won World Junior Cross Country Championship

1993–96: studied French, German and Economics at Loughborough University while competing at an international level

1995–2002: gradually ran longer and longer races – 5000m, 10,000m track races, half-marathons and marathons

2000: married Gary Lough

2002: awarded an **M.B.E.** by the Queen

2004: dropped out of the marathon and the 10,000m race at the Athens Olympics

2005: won London marathon in a new world record time

Historical biographies

When you read about the conditions of historical figures, be careful! Some conditions were described by the people themselves, or by people they knew. Others, however, have been **diagnosed** after their death – in some cases, centuries after the person was alive.

Pliny (Gaius Plinius Secundis) the Elder (Italy AD 23-79)

Pliny the Elder wrote historical and scientific works, including a thirty-seven volume encyclopedia of the natural sciences.

Pliny had bad **asthma**. We know because he and his friends wrote about it: for example, Pliny wrote that smoking coltsfoot leaves helped bad coughs. His nephew described how Pliny died during an eruption of Mount Vesuvius. Pliny could not get enough air into his sick lungs and suffocated in the volcano's fumes.

Today the term 'Plinian' describes a very violent volcanic eruption.

We can say with some certainty that Pliny had asthma because it was a known condition in Roman times. A Greek doctor, Hippocrates, first described asthma in about 500 BC. The word comes from the Greek and means 'laboured breathing'.

Isaac Newton (UK 1643-1727)

Newton, scientist and astronomer, 'discovered' gravity and wrote laws about the way things move. People who knew him wrote that he had some **fits**. Today some people say he had **epilepsy**, others argue that his fits were not epileptic. Without the patient, it is difficult to make a proper diagnosis.

Ludwig van Beethoven (Germany 1770-1827)

Many written accounts from Beethoven's time tell of how this composer gradually went **deaf**. He wrote his last symphony when he had gone completely deaf.

It is easier to find solid proof that a historical person had some conditions, e.g. **deafness**, than others, e.g. **epilepsy**.

Other conditions however were not described so early in history. **Dyslexia** was not recognised until the late 19th century.

Leonardo da Vinci (Italy 1452–1519)

Leonardo was born near the town of Vinci. During his life, Leonardo got jobs as a painter, sculptor, military architect and engineer. He is best known for his paintings, which include the *Mona Lisa*. To draw people well, he dissected **corpses** to see their muscles.

Leonardo was an inventor, too. He drew plans for a robot, a helicopter and other inventions which would not be made for over 500 years.

Leonardo sometimes wrote backwards, from right to left, so you can only read it when you hold a mirror up beside it. This may have been because he was left-handed and would have smudged his quill's ink with his hand, or it could have been a basic form of code to hide his ideas from others.

In the 20th century some people diagnosed Leonardo as suffering from **dyslexia**. One of the ways of telling if a person is dyslexic is by seeing if they spell incorrectly, or if they write words back to front. Leonardo did both. But Leonardo was constantly changing between mirror writing and normal writing, so perhaps it is not surprising that he sometimes got mixed up. Also, in that period spelling was not fixed as it is today – Shakespeare (1564–1616) spelled words differently all the time.

So, was Leonardo dyslexic? We'll only know if someone invents a time machine and goes back to test him – just the sort of invention he might have thought up himself!

Composers and Musicians

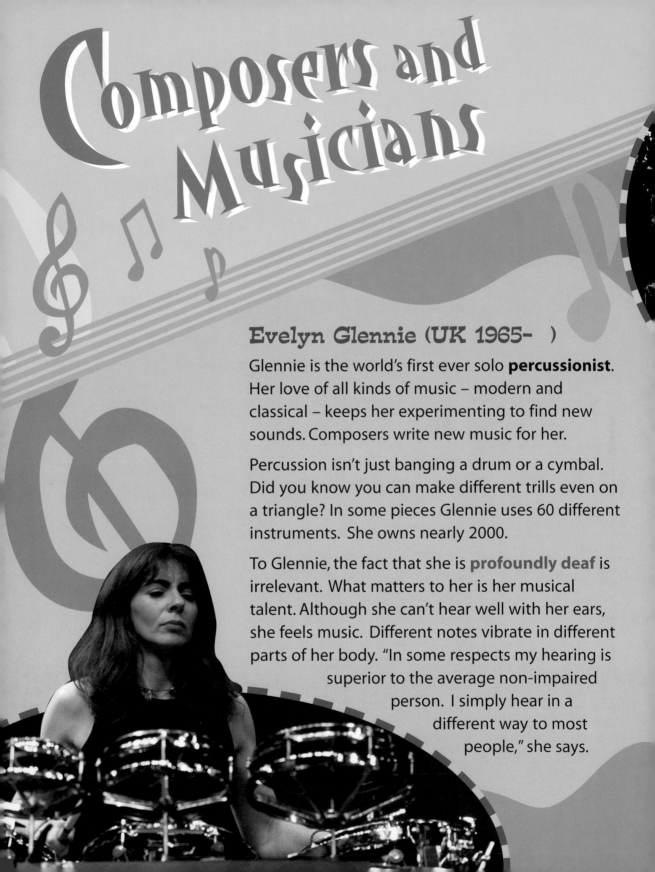

Evelyn Glennie (UK 1965-)

Glennie is the world's first ever solo **percussionist**. Her love of all kinds of music – modern and classical – keeps her experimenting to find new sounds. Composers write new music for her.

Percussion isn't just banging a drum or a cymbal. Did you know you can make different trills even on a triangle? In some pieces Glennie uses 60 different instruments. She owns nearly 2000.

To Glennie, the fact that she is **profoundly deaf** is irrelevant. What matters to her is her musical talent. Although she can't hear well with her ears, she feels music. Different notes vibrate in different parts of her body. "In some respects my hearing is superior to the average non-impaired person. I simply hear in a different way to most people," she says.

Bare feet help Glennie feel vibrations through the floor.

Evelyn Glennie

Born: Aberdeen, UK, 19 July 1965

Studied: Ellon Academy, Aberdeenshire and the Royal College of Music, London

1973: Age 8: best marks in the UK for Grade 1 piano exam. Nerve damage began to affect her hearing

1977: hearing almost gone – taught to 'hear' through her body

1988: won first Grammy award

1993: awarded an **O.B.E.** by the Queen

1994: married Greg Malcangi

Present: Glennie plays all over the world, solo and with major orchestras and conductors

Glennie points out that if she chose to she could be upset that her hands weren't bigger, which might be helpful for playing instruments. But no one feels she has a 'handicap' because she doesn't have big hands. So why would anyone feel that her deafness was a handicap?

Antonio Vivaldi
(Italy 1678-1741)

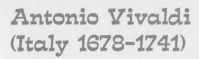

Vivaldi was a priest, but in 1704 he stopped giving services because the church **incense** made his **asthma** bad.

Instead, he got a job teaching violin and music at the Pieta, the girls' **orphanage** in Venice. His first collection of music for their orchestra was published in 1705.

Music lovers from all over Europe came to hear Vivaldi's famous concerts. In 1713 he was made Music Master.

Vivaldi enjoyed travelling, but as he grew older his asthma got worse, and he could hardly walk a couple of metres without stopping.

In 1740 he went to Vienna, Austria, possibly to work for Emperor Charles VI. But the Emperor died almost as soon as Vivaldi arrived, and Vivaldi died there, poor and alone, in 1741.

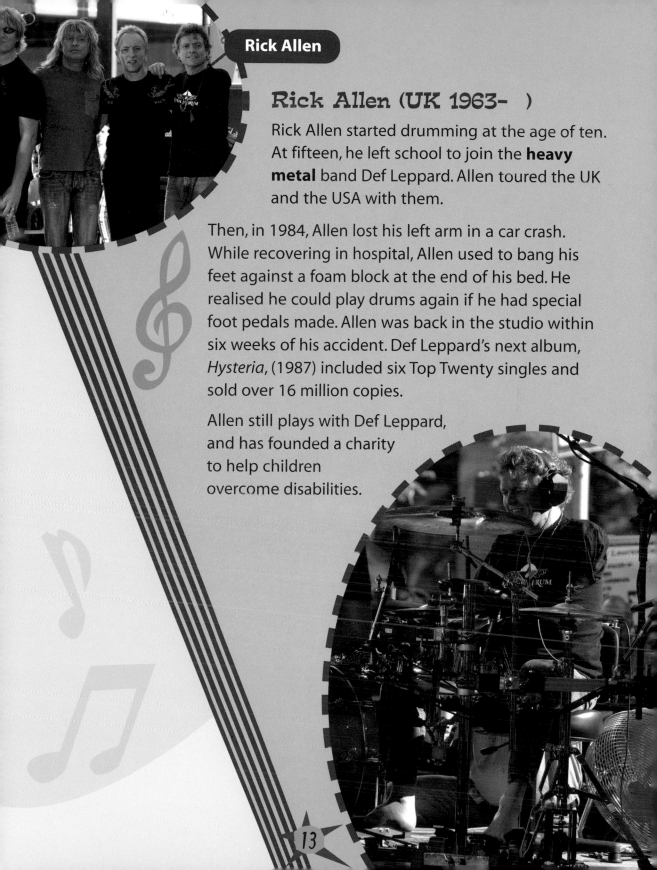

Rick Allen (UK 1963-)

Rick Allen started drumming at the age of ten. At fifteen, he left school to join the **heavy metal** band Def Leppard. Allen toured the UK and the USA with them.

Then, in 1984, Allen lost his left arm in a car crash. While recovering in hospital, Allen used to bang his feet against a foam block at the end of his bed. He realised he could play drums again if he had special foot pedals made. Allen was back in the studio within six weeks of his accident. Def Leppard's next album, *Hysteria*, (1987) included six Top Twenty singles and sold over 16 million copies.

Allen still plays with Def Leppard, and has founded a charity to help children overcome disabilities.

Politicians

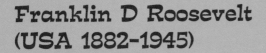

Franklin D Roosevelt (USA 1882–1945)

Roosevelt was President of the United States of America from 1933–1945.

In his thirties, Roosevelt wanted to become a politician. When he was crippled with **polio** in 1921, he was convinced that he wouldn't get elected if he appeared weak. So he never used a wheelchair in public, but walked with the help of a bodyguard.

At the time Roosevelt became President, in 1933, unemployment was very high. Roosevelt introduced the 'New Deal' – laws which he hoped would pull the country out of economic depression.

Roosevelt (right) in 1945, with the UK's Prime Minister, Winston Churchill. Churchill had dyslexia and suffered from depression.

The Second World War began in 1939, and in 1941, when Japan attacked America directly, Roosevelt led the USA in joining Britain and other **allies** to fight against Germany and Japan.

Roosevelt's health got worse during the difficult war years, and he died only weeks before the war ended. He was the USA's longest-serving president, having been elected four times.

David Blunkett
(UK 1947-)

Blind since birth, Blunkett was told at school that he would only ever get a low-paid, manual job. He joined the **Labour Party** and rose to become a senior politician in the British government at the turn of the 21st century.

Margaret Wilson
(New Zealand 1947-)

An outspoken politician, Wilson very quickly climbed the ladder of New Zealand politics to become the speaker of the parliament. A lawyer, she has also held the post of Attorney- General. Wilson had one leg **amputated** after a battle with **cancer**.

Actors

Sarah Bernhardt (France 1844–1923)

Bernhardt was the most famous actress of the 19th century, performing all over Europe and in the USA.

In 1915, Bernhardt injured her leg so badly in one performance that she had to have it cut off. But, within months she was acting again, and she continued working on stage and screen until her death.

The story goes…After her leg was **amputated** someone sent her a telegram offering her $100,000 to put her leg on show in an exhibition in the USA. Bernhardt sent a reply: "Which leg?"

Sylvester Stallone (USA 1946–)

Stallone's trademark snarl and slurred speech are the result of birth complications which left the left side of his face **paralysed**.

Action hero Stallone starred in the *Rocky* movies.

16

Michael J Fox (Canada 1961-)

Fox started acting professionally at the age of fifteen. He has won many awards for his work in TV and films, which include the *Back to the Future* trilogy (1985–90).

In 1991, Fox discovered he had Parkinson's disease, but he didn't tell the public until 1998. He carried on working on his TV comedy series, *Spin City*, until 2000. More recently, he has voiced several cartoons, including *Stuart Little*.

Fox, the voice of Stuart Little.

Marilyn Monroe (USA 1926-1962)

Marilyn Monroe had a mild stutter, possibly because of her troubled childhood – she went to an orphanage and was fostered by more than ten different families. Her low, breathy voice may have been the result of techniques she learned to stop the stuttering.

Monroe, film star of the 1950s

Para-athletes

Para-**athletes** are sportspeople who compete against other athletes with the same level of disability as themselves. Sports include wheelchair basketball, blind judo, shooting, table tennis and swimming. Para-athletes compete internationally in many competitions, including the Paralympics, which take place every four years, just after the Olympic Games.

Lucy Ogechukwu Ejike (Nigeria 1977-   )

2004 Paralympic powerlifting gold medallist, Ejike lifts weights from her wheelchair.

Marlon Shirley (USA 1978-)

Abandoned as a three-year-old, at five Shirley had an accident with a lawn mower at his **orphanage** that cost him his lower leg. He has risen above his problems to become the fastest **amputee** in the world for four years running.

The first 'games for the **paralysed**' in 1948 were only for people who were *para*lysed, but the 'para' in paralympics now takes the meaning of '*para*llel' – the games are beside and equal to the Olympic games. In the 2004 Paralympics in Athens, 3,900 para-athletes competed in 19 different sports.

Tanni Grey-Thompson (UK 1969-)

Enthusiastic and determined, Grey-Thompson is one of the world's best para-athletes. Having been born with **spina bifida** and paralysed from the waist down, she is a record-breaking wheelchair racer with 11 Paralympic gold medals. The Queen appointed her Dame Tanni in 2005 for services to sport.

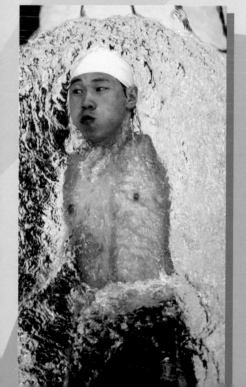

Junquan He (China 1970-)

In the Athens Paralympic Games 2004, China was the winning country, with 63 gold medals. Junquan He won four swimming gold medals in his disability class. He lost both arms when he received a bad electric shock at the age of three.

He was awarded Sportsperson of the Year with a Disability in China in 2005.

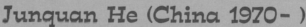

Mario Lemieux
(Canada 1965-)

2002 Olympic gold medallist, Lemieux is the sixth highest scoring ice hockey player in the world.

Lemieux was gifted at hockey from a very early age. In 1984 he was the best newcomer for the US professional leagues and was picked by the Pittsburgh Penguins team. Lemieux's scoring saw him among the top players for the next nine years, and he was tipped to become the world's number one.

But, in 1993, Lemieux was diagnosed with **Hodgkin's disease**, a type of **cancer**. He had to take time off for **radiation treatment**. Amazingly, he missed only twenty-four games in that season and came back to be the highest scorer of the season! Lemieux won his battle with cancer and continued to play at the highest level until 1997, when he retired.

But, in 1999, his team was going through a bad patch, and Lemieux came to the rescue. He came out of retirement to help buy the team and returned to the ice to take it to the top of the league as a player/owner.

> 'Super Mario' has an average score of 0.805 goals per game – the highest ever score in America's National Hockey League.

Lemieux might have become the top ice hockey player in the world if he hadn't missed so many games through illness. But what he has achieved is in some ways more impressive.

Redgrave won Olympic gold rowing medals in 1984, 1988, 1992, 1996 and 2000.

Steve Redgrave (UK 1962-)

Redgrave is one of only five Olympians to win gold medals at each of five consecutive Olympic Games. Redgrave is driven to succeed and has fought against several conditions to hit his goals: dyslexia, colitis, diabetes.

Artists

Vincent Van Gogh
(The Netherlands 1853–1890)

Van Gogh worked as an art dealer, a teacher and a preacher before his brother encouraged him to become an artist in 1880.

He travelled Europe, studying paintings with various artists. In 1886 a group of artists he met in Paris inspired him to create pictures in dots or stripes of paint. He moved to the south of France in 1888, where he painted some of his best work, including his Sunflower paintings.

Van Gogh suffered from **depression**, which got worse through his life. He spent more and more time in mental hospitals, though he still painted. In 1890, very depressed, he shot himself in the chest and died two days later.

Self Portrait with Bandaged Ear, 1889

He only sold one painting in his lifetime and often went without food to buy painting equipment instead. His mental health is reflected in his wild brushstrokes.

Starry Night, 1889

Frida Kahlo
(Magdalena Carmen Frida Kahlo y Calderón)
(Mexico 1907–1954)

Kahlo got **polio** at six, which left her with a withered right leg. Then at the age of 18 a bus accident left her close to death. Her spine, pelvis and other bones were broken, including 11 breaks in her right leg. Kahlo began painting while she recovered from the accident, using a special easel which attached to her bed.

In 1929, Kahlo married an older artist, who encouraged her to build on her Mexican heritage. She began to wear ethnic clothes and paint in a Mexican folk-art style.

Kahlo was in constant pain all her life and had over 30 operations to correct her injuries. In 1953 her right leg was **amputated**. Confined to a wheelchair, she became very unhappy and died the next year at the age of 44.

> **Kahlo painted over 50 self-portraits. Her work explored the themes of death, the role of women, and her mixed-race Mexican/German background.**

Dr Temple Grandin (USA 1947-)

Grandin has **autism**. She didn't begin to talk until she was three and a half. As a child she found it hard to communicate and was a problem child. People at her school called her 'weird'. But one teacher recognised her abilities and helped her to continue her education. Grandin went to three Universities and studied animal science. She became particularly interested in looking after **livestock**.

With the help of medicines, Grandin was able to control the worst effects of her condition, and she learned that some aspects of her autism were useful in her work.

Grandin is now a university professor in the USA, teaching students about how livestock behave. She also designs stock pens and runs which keep livestock calm and relaxed and encourage them to go in the right direction.

Grandin's autism makes her think in pictures. This helps her imagine how animals might think. When she was designing a cattle dip, Grandin imagined what being a cow was like. She took lots of videos of cattle runs and cattle dips from cow-eye level to see what the cattle saw and what might frighten them.

A cattle run from a cow's point of view.

Farmers use livestock chutes for many reasons, for example, to sort animals, to give them medicine, to dip them or to get them on to lorries.

Grandin realised that animals would prefer to walk into a chute that was curved, so that they would think they had come back round to where they had come from. She also realised they would feel more relaxed if the walls were solid, so that they would not be bothered by movement all around them.

Scientists

John Goodricke (UK 1764–1786)

Profoundly deaf Goodricke became an amateur **astronomer** when the father of a friend invited him to use his private observatory.

We see Algol as one star, but it is two stars revolving round each other

Algol looks dim to us when the dim star is nearest.

Algol looks bright to us when the bright star is nearest

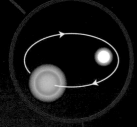

One of the mysteries of the night sky at the time was why the brightness of some stars changed over time. In 1782, when he was only eighteen, Goodricke suggested that a star called Algol was really two stars going round each other.

He received a medal from the **Royal Society** in 1783 for his work. Goodricke died suddenly, probably of **pneumonia**, and never found out that the Society had just made him a member.

It was another 100 years later before his ideas were proved to be correct.

Stephen Hawking (UK 1942-)

Hawking combines astronomy, maths and physics to study the universe. He has researched **black holes**, the beginning, and the end of time.

Hawking is famous because he has written about these ideas in a way that makes them (almost!) understandable to non-scientists.

Hawking was at university studying physics when he started getting clumsy. He was diagnosed with **motor neurone disease** at the age of 21 and the disease got slowly worse. By the age of 32, Hawking needed help with eating and getting out of bed. He was confined to a wheelchair. Hawking's speech became more and more slurred until an operation in 1985 left him unable to talk at all. After that, Hawking got his first 'talking computer'.

Hawking still studies the universe. In 2004 he presented a new idea for how black holes worked. This new idea went against some of his old work, but Hawking was not afraid to admit that he had changed his mind.

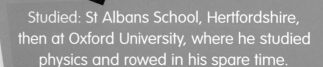

Born: Oxford, UK, 8th January 1942

Studied: St Albans School, Hertfordshire, then at Oxford University, where he studied physics and rowed in his spare time.

1962: moved to Cambridge University to do further research

1963: first diagnosed with motor neurone disease. Given three years to live

1953 married first wife, Jane Wilde (divorced 1990). They have three children

1971: did the maths to show that the **Big Bang** idea of the start of the universe could work

1985: operation means Hawking cannot speak and needs 24 hour nursing care

1988: wrote 'A Brief History of Time'

1988: made a **Companion of Honour** by the Queen

1995: married second wife, Elaine Mason

27

Glossary of conditions

AMPUTATION To have all or part of a limb cut off. Someone who has had a limb cut off is an amputee.

ASTHMA During an asthma attack your lungs' airways get narrower, and sometimes they get sticky with mucus. This makes it hard to breathe. An asthma attack can be set off by something that you are allergic to, e.g. dog hair, pollen.

AUTISM Autism is a mental condition which stops you responding normally to the world around you and makes it difficult for you to express yourself in words. Autistic people can be very gifted in other ways, e.g. in mathematics.

BLINDNESS Blindness affects your vision. It can be caused by problems in your eyes; in the nerves that send messages to your brain; or in the part of the brain that works out what you're looking at. A visual impairment means that you have some loss of vision. A fully blind person is unable to see anything.

CANCER Cancer causes your body to make cells that are not normal. These cells grow very quickly and take over normal cells. They can spread to other parts of the body. Cancer can start in many parts of the body, e.g. lung cancer, bone cancer.

COLITIS Colitis is an inflammation of the walls of your colon, which is the last part of your digestive system.

DEAFNESS Deafness affects your hearing. It can be caused by problems in your ears; in the nerves that send messages to your brain; or in the part of the brain that works out what you're listening to. A hearing impairment means that you have some loss of hearing. Profoundly deaf means that you have hardly any hearing at all.

DEPRESSION Feeling sad and hopeless for a long time and rarely feeling happy. Depression can be caused by something outside a person – the death of a loved one, for example – or it can be caused by something inside the brain not working properly.

DIABETES When you have diabetes, your body can't use the sugar in your food properly. Your body doesn't make enough of the chemicals which control the way sugars are broken down and used as energy.

DYSLEXIA Dyslexia is a difficulty in being able to read and spell words. Dyslexia is not related to intelligence, and dyslexics can be very talented in other ways. Symptoms include slow reading, mixing up letters, finding it difficult to sound out words and writing words with letters mixed up.

EPILEPSY A disease of the nerves in the brain which causes convulsions – violent fits where the body moves uncontrollably.

HODGKIN'S DISEASE Hodgkin's disease is a cancer of the lymph system in the body. Lymph is a fluid that the body makes to help it fight diseases.

MOTOR NEURONE DISEASES Motor neurone diseases are when the nerves in the body slowly stop working, so the muscles they control become weak. You can become paralysed and have problems swallowing, speaking and breathing.

PARALYSIS Being unable to move or feel anything. Paralysis can occur as the result of many different diseases and conditions. You can have paralysis of just one part of your body, or of many parts.

PARKINSON'S DISEASE Parkinson's disease breaks down brain cells which tell the body's nervous system what to do. Hands shake, then movement and balance become affected. Over time sufferers can have trouble talking, swallowing and even smiling.

PNEUMONIA A serious disease of the lungs. This infection can be treated with antibiotics if it is caught early enough.

POLIO Polio is a highly infectious disease caused by a virus which attacks your nervous system. Your legs become paralysed, and in bad cases your whole body is paralysed.

SPINA BIFIDA Spina bifida is a condition in which you are born with an opening in your spine. Your main nerves are protected inside your spine, so if there is an opening, nerves can be damaged and you can be paralysed.

STUTTER To stutter is to keep repeating the sounds at the beginnings of words.

Glossary

allies – people or countries on the same side in a war

astronomer – someone who studies the universe and the stars

athlete – someone who does physical exercise

Big Bang – an idea about how the universe began 15 million years ago

black hole – a region in space with such strong gravity that no light escapes

Companion of Honour – a title that the British Queen can give to people who have achieved something very special

condition – the state in which something in the body is not normal, or does not behave normally, e.g. *she has a heart condition*

corpses – dead bodies

diagnose – to find out what disease or condition someone has got by finding out what symptoms they have

fits – sudden violent, jerky movements of the body and limbs

heavy metal – a loud kind of rock music

incense – a burning substance which makes a spicy smell

Labour Party – one of the political parties in the United Kingdom

livestock – farm animals

M.B.E. – 'Member of the Order of the British Empire' – an honour and title the British Queen can give to people who have achieved something special

O.B.E. – 'Officer of the Order of the British Empire' – an honour and title the British Queen can give to people who have achieved something special

orphanage – a home for children whose parents are dead

percussionist – someone who plays musical instruments which are played by being struck or shaken

radiation treatment – to treat a disease by trying to kill it with radioactive energy

Royal Society – an organisation of academic people in London dedicated to promoting Science

Index